The views and opinions in this book are exactly that views and opinions.

They are my views and opinions that formed over the years from m experiences. Firstly from mv in mainstream education home educating my spent many twilight researching the scienc children learn as I find it fa ...lls research, along with watching ...ldren grow forms the basis for this book.

# rebel

*verb*

verb: **rebel**; 3rd person present: **rebels**; past tense: **rebelled**; past participle: **rebelled**; gerund or present participle: **rebelling**

/rɪˈbɛl/

resist authority, control, or convention.

"respect did not prevent children from rebelling against their parents"

*antonyms: obey, conform*

FOR MY REBEL GIRLS WHOM I LOOK UPON
WITH WONDER IN MUCH THE SAME WAY,
THEY LOOK UPON THE WORLD.

# "EVERYTHING YOU WANT IS ON THE OTHER SIDE OF FEAR"

*jack canfield*

# LETTER FROM A MOTHER

A piece of me has always felt a little bit lost in motherhood. From the very beginning, I did things differently to most of the people around me. I co-slept, cuddled, 'made a rod for my own back'. "They'll never learn" people would advise me.

I chose to connect instead of punishing. Cuddle instead of leaving them to cry it out. I chose to be honest. I chose to extend to my children the same respect and choices that I offered to adults.

But I became a little misguided when it came to our decisions surrounding education. I wasn't one of those mums who was excited at the prospect of sending our children to school. I did so with a heavy heart and reluctantly went back to work full time.

I wasn't happy, my life was not filling me with joy and satisfaction. When I was at home I was panicking about work and when I was at work I was stressing about home.

But I could have coped with this if my children were happy. Sadly, they were not. My eldest daughter hated school from day one.

I was one of those mums who would drive to work in tears every morning as I had left her screaming at the door, being 'comforted' by the rather stressed out teacher. Things began to gradually worsen as the year progressed. Our beautiful, bright, bubbly little girl became introverted, quiet and very, very angry. Her eating suffered, her sleeping suffered and she was very down in herself. At her lowest, she vomited several times a day at school. People were quick to say "It's just her age." "It's just a stage she's going through." Or my favourite: "She'll grow out of it." Well, she didn't grow out of it. A trip to the GP confirmed our suspicions. Our daughter was suffering from anxiety, probably caused by school. This is quite common according to the doctor, particularly since schools have felt the need to heap a ton of pressure on children at a younger and younger age.

This fact makes my heart feel so sad, why are we allowing, no forcing, our children to become stressed and anxious at the tender age of 5. We had to do something, which is where our journey into home educating began.

I am now all about making our life learning as fun, exciting and engaging as I can. I'm giving my girls their childhood back, helping shape them into thoughtful, honest and curious citizens and making so many precious memories along the way.

I am so passionate about unschooling because it works. I have had the privilege and joy of watching my children unfold, becoming complex humans without being moulded and shaped to fit a certain role. It's messy and it is beautiful in all of its breath-taking chaos.

I have written this book in the hopes it will hold someone's hand through the trepidation of deciding to home educate their children. To inspire people to know that life can be joyous and fun. You don't have to struggle on trying to live up to societies expectations of your life.

You can choose to live a slow, joy-filled, peaceful life alongside your children.

I wrote this book to be the book I needed to read in those early days when I was filled with so much self-doubt. It is written in two parts.

'Part 1: The What' aims to inform you and help you understand what the principle of unschooling is, how children really learn and why people choose this lifestyle.

'Part 2: The How' is there to arm you with the tools you need to guide your children and help them to reach their full potential.

Writing this book has been a labour of love, and a dream of mine brought to life. I hope it helps you to create a magical childhood for your children filled with imagination, curiosity, and wonder.

peace and love
natalie x

# PART ONE: THE WHAT

# "EDUCATION IS NOT PREPARATION FOR LIFE - EDUCATION IS LIFE ITSELF"

*john dewey*

# LIFE WITHOUT SCHOOL

Let's start at the beginning, what is Home Education? In its simplest form, it is exactly that, living your life without school being a part of it. Making the decision to educate your children in your home setting.

As with all things in life, there is no right or wrong way to home educate, or home-school, your children. Some families choose to replicate school at home following a curriculum, lesson plans, and strict routines. Other parents home educate for cultural or religious reasons and teach their children within the specific limits of their beliefs. Others, like us, choose to unschool.

"Unschooling, what is that?" I hear you cry. Unschooling, also known as child-led learning, is not just an academic philosophy or 'method of education'. It is a way of life. It means offering your children the same choices and respect that you would extend to other adults. It means learning through life. Treating every second of every day as a new learning experience filled with joy and wonder.

Don't your children just scoff sweets and binge watch TV all day? Now hold on just a moment, I said "unschooling" not "unparenting". The biggest myth surrounding unschooling is that unschooled children have no limits.

They will eat ice-cream for breakfast, play on their iPads all day and night, and grow up to become benefit scrounging losers who are unable to string a sentence together. This is the biggest load of baloney I have ever heard and unfortunately provides the fuel for all of the negative media attention that home education receives.

All parents have limits, am I right? It would be foolish as a parent not to set your own limits and boundaries. Unschooling parents are always there helping, guiding, listening, and being very involved in their children's lives. The difference in an unschooling familial relationship is that the boundaries and limits are not enforced in an authoritarian manner using punishments.

To define it in its simplest terms, unschooling is choosing not to send your children to school, and also not to replicate school at home. Unschooling is the complete opposite of mainstream schooling and a rejection of the limits and concepts that traditional schooling stands for.

# "ONE TEST OF THE CORRECTNESS OF EDUCATIONAL PROCEDURE IS THE HAPPINESS OF THE CHILD"

*maria montessori*

# FAILINGS OF THE SYSTEM

Before I begin to elaborate on the failings of our current education system, I should clarify that as a family we are not anti-school. School will always have a place in society. Not everyone has the privilege to be able to home educate (and it is a huge privilege), and not everyone wants to home educate. For those reasons, school will always be needed. However, it is my belief that the reason there has been a surge in home education in recent years is that parents are becoming fed up with a system that is letting a profound number of children down and fails to progress with the times. Educating your children at home is a complete lifestyle choice. Even though I am passionate about it, I understand that society needs schools. Some children thrive at school, others simply have terrible home situations meaning that school is their sanctuary. As a society, we have an obligation to make sure we are giving children the education and experiences that they deserve if they're going to be spending 13 years of their life at school.

What is wrong with mainstream education? The decision to home educate isn't one parents take lightly. If you are reading this book you are either considering unschooling or you are already walking the path of life without school.

Firstly, you should know that unschooling means you are going against a mainstream idea that is so deeply ingrained in our culture that you are constantly battling against people's questioning and narrow-minded opinions. Someone must be at home with the children which often means living on one wage, or two part-time wages. Couple this with no free school meals, buying your own equipment, paying for activities and trips, and extortionate exam fees; home educating can soon seriously dent a family's budget.

Why would I want to send my children to school? Currently, UK schools are ranked as some of the lowest in the developed world, I'm afraid we don't even make the top 20 for English and maths. We have even dropped rankings in the last 3 years.

Teachers suffering from mental health problems are at an all-time high. In a recent YouGov survey of education professionals, 79% said they experienced psychological, physical or behavioural symptoms because of work. More than three quarters, 77%, said that poor teacher mental health was having a detrimental effect on pupils' progress. Almost one in five (19%) said they had experienced panic attacks. Over half (56%) had suffered from insomnia and difficulties sleeping and over a third (41%) had trouble concentrating. Last year alone, 35,000 teachers left their jobs for reasons other than retirement [1]. I'm not sure I'm comfortable leaving my children in the care of stressed-out adults when they can be at home surrounded by positive influences. Friends and families who care about them.

Tell me again why school is better? It must be the socialisation thing that everyone always bleats on about whenever the phrase 'home education' is mentioned.

In the UK on average there are 16000 children and young people absent from school due to bullying. Over half of all LGBTQ young people have experienced homophobic bullying. 45% of children and young people will experience bullying at school [2]. Despite what some people say being bullied is not a rite of passage, and in no way is it character building. All human beings are worthy and deserve to be treated with respect. Unschooled children choose their friends, who span a wide age range. You wouldn't stand for bullying in the workplace as an adult, yet it seems so readily accepted as part of school life.

What about monitoring the academic progress of home educated children? For us, and many other parents, the main reason we have chosen to live a life without school is to get as far away as possible from standardised tests and assessments. We want our children to be defined by more than the boxes they tick. We want them to be free to progress at their own pace and not feel pressurised into learning things too soon. We never want them to be told or made to feel like they are just not quite good enough.

There are some shocking statistics about anxiety and depression surrounding SATS for primary aged children. A survey of 1,200 teachers found that cases of stress, anxiety, and panic attacks have increased in more than three-quarters (78%) of primary schools over the past two years. In addition, school leaders reported an increase in fear of academic failure (76%) and depression (55%) among their pupils in the period since 2014 [4]. These figures make for pretty sad reading.

And if primary school doesn't mess up their mental wellbeing then let's take a look at the figures for secondary education. Whilst researching this book I came across a report aptly named 'Exam

Factories'. I found this quote particularly poignant:

*"It is crucial that it is recognised that the current system of measuring pupils' attainment and using this to judge schools and teachers is deeply damaging to children and young people, and does not foster the skills and talents that are needed in higher education or in employment, or the attributes that will be valued in future citizens. An urgent review of current accountability measures should take place, with a view to substantially changing them."*

In May 2016 Childline delivered more than 3000 counselling sessions due to exam stress [5]. Self-harm in teenagers has risen by 68% in the last 3 years [6]. And if that isn't jaw-dropping enough for you, the suicide rates for children in the UK aged between 10 and 14 is at its highest in 14 years [7].

I think I've thrown enough facts and figures in the mix to satisfy the people who need hard evidence that schools just aren't working (and to be quite honest I'm sick of researching them because it hurts my heart).

So aside from all of the shocking facts, and the exams, and the bullying and the ridiculous times tables tests at age 8 and spelling tests for 4-year-olds.

What is the actual aim of school? Most people would say it is to prepare children for their working lives. Let's take a little look into the future. Because from what I can see we are in a rapidly advancing world. The current education system still uses the Dickensian system of sitting behind a desk all day, mainly focusing on maths and literacy which was designed in the industrial revolution to create a generation of factory workers. All the while schools are cutting funding for sports, arts and technology.

I'm not sure how this archaic system proposes to produce creative, imaginative, passionate, driven workers. Because all I can see is a generation of children being taught to pass exams to enable their schools to look good on a league table, and little else.

No thanks, not for the merry band of unschooling families! We would rather our children not know their times tables but be competent in real skills. Passionate about learning new things and immersing themselves in different cultures. Learning in the real world. Not trapped behind a desk in a dank, artificially lit classroom, being lectured by a teacher who is too stressed to inspire passion.

This brings me nicely onto the whitewashing of the traditional school curriculum. If you take a look at the curriculum that is taught in school you might be surprised to learn that children today are still studying the same things that I learned in the eighties. The curriculum has failed to progress with the times. The history curriculum in particular seems to focus on one-sided events, glorifying topics such as the British Empire, colonisation and World Wars, instead of teaching a broader multi-faceted real version of events. Unschooled children are free to pursue their interests instead of ticking off the learning objectives set by the current government and whatever agendas they have during their time in power.

When the government can provide schools that do not damage the mental health of our youngsters. When they can offer all children a tailored, superior education. Then maybe unschooling will cease to exist.

As controversial as these views may seem, the current state of mainstream education is such that unschooling is a rapidly growing movement. Yes, home education isn't for everyone, but it is for us.

As an aside let us think about the children who need to be at school, who don't have that choice. Let's fight to make schools better for them.

# "I WANT FREEDOM FOR THE FULL EXPRESSION OF MY PERSONALITY"

*mahatma gandhi*

# MY BODY, MY CHOICE

Autonomy is the most integral part of unschooling. Unschooling without giving your children full autonomy over their learning is not unschooling at all.

What is autonomy? Autonomy is when you have control over your time, bodies, and minds. Mainstream schooling and even societies expectations of parenting are firmly against this idea. The majority of adults believe that all decisions about a child and their life are the right of the parent. From how they dress, to what they eat, when they sleep, what hobbies they participate in, to complete control of their personal possessions, and even their bodies. Bodily autonomy is a basic human right and children are humans too, they deserve the same autonomy extended to adults in society. Autonomy and unschooling go hand in hand, it means modelling respectful parenting and giving children the freedom to express themselves however they please. In doing this we can raise strong, confident humans who will respect others choices and autonomy too.

What does autonomy look like? Autonomy means trusting children to make decisions about their lives. Allowing them to choose what they wear, how much they eat, who they give their affection to, what happens to their possessions and gives them complete control over their bodies. As I stated in an earlier chapter this does not mean "unparenting". There are, of course, limits and boundaries but mostly there is respect and trust. Mainstream society seems to believe that you have to choose between one or the other, strict control or total neglect.

Why don't people trust their children? Many people are so terrified to give their children too much freedom because it may mean they no longer have any influence over them, they command 'respect' but what they really want is 'obedience'. When your relationship with your children is based on mutual trust and respect from giving them complete autonomy you actually have more influence over the decisions they make.

As an unschooling family, you do not work against your children, you work with them. It's not a parenting struggle where you're battling with your children, you are a team. Unschooling means respecting one another, listening, giving your children advice. When children are not constantly restricted, forced and coerced they are more likely to listen to you as a parent when it really matters. If they fear punishment, they are less likely to confide in you when they need to. The key is to model good decision making and behaviour to your children whilst living life alongside them. Children are constantly learning and who better to learn from than the people who care about them the most.

Children are not inherently bad. In fact, it is quite the opposite. Children have a natural desire to learn, to please people, they want to be good and make people happy.

We have been conditioned to believe that children, without adult control, will be 'bad', 'naughty', constantly want to make the wrong choices. Children are not believed to be capable, people assume that they would never adequately learn anything on their own. It is assumed that children need coercion, force, punishment, and constant direction in order to achieve anything.

What happens when you give your children complete autonomy? They run around naked, never bathe, eat copious amounts of junk food, swear at passers-by and play on computer games all day long! Jokes, this is not what happens when you give your children autonomy. This is what happens when you 'unparent', not when you unschool. Unschooling parents must be deeply involved in their children's lives. The result of mixing together autonomy and respectful parenting, learning through life together is a wonderful life filled with an innate sense of joy and wonder.

We trust that our babies will learn to walk, to eat, to sleep, to communicate and talk all without the involvement of an institutionalised educational setting. So why does our trust in children end at age 4? Do they suddenly lose the ability to learn from the environment around them? No, we have just been conditioned for so long as a society to believe that the only way our children will learn is in a government institution. That the only things valuable enough to learn are a dictated to us from a prescribed, rigid curriculum developed by men in suits with an agenda.

It is time to trust our children again, to value their natural curiosity and drive to learn, to rebel against a system that no longer works.
When we give them our trust and allow children full autonomy, beautiful, magical things happen.

# "WHEN YOU TEACH A CHILD SOMETHING YOU TAKE AWAY FOREVER HIS CHANCE OF DISCOVERING IT FOR HIMSELF"

*jean piaget*

# A DESIRE TO LEARN

The biggest myth people believe about children is that without school they would not want to learn. This simply is not true. As parents, we've all been through what I like to call the 'why stage'. You know, when kids ask a million questions about everything, "But why Mama?" feels like a broken record played on repeat all day.

Children are born with a natural desire to learn. A curiosity to explore the world around them and absorb any and all information they can get their hands on like little sponges. Do you know what kills this innate desire to find stuff out for themselves? We do. Us adults who 'know it all' and 'know what is best for the child'.

The quickest way to kill a joyful spark of curiosity is to take away that joy and wonder of discovery. Forcing a child to learn something in a prescribed way and not allowing them to discover the answers for themselves squashes all of their natural learning instincts.

How many of us found a subject boring at school, only to rediscover the joy in that subject when we were left to stumble upon it ourselves in adulthood? I despised history and geography at school, my teachers were boring and had us copying paragraphs out of a textbook in complete silence. This was what they called 'learning'. I can tell you now the only thing I learned during those lessons was how much finger cramp hurts from gripping your pen too tightly. But as an adult, I have rediscovered history and geography. I have digested so many books about historical events and stood in awe of monuments built by past civilisations. I have grown to love the natural world and educated myself on how our beautiful, fragile planet works. If I retook my GCSE's now I know I would fail. I got grade A in French, but can barely string together a few sentences. In short, all school taught me was how to retain enough information to pass an exam, the price is that it also killed my natural desire to learn.

As soon as you start school you are told that you need to be taught. But not the things important to you, and never at your own pace. You must be taught the things that the people in charge deem important enough for you to learn, despite the fact they don't know anything about you. You are told you are not good enough until you reach a certain standard, that someone in authority made up. You must reach this standard within a specific timeframe, that someone in authority made up. You are never seen as capable, you couldn't possibly learn enough on your own volition. Eventually, you will come to believe this of yourself, that you are no longer capable of self-directed learning. That the only way to learn is by doing as you are told by someone with more power than you.

The way children are taught at school is very different from how unschoolers learn. Unschooled children are given the freedom to trust their instincts and follow their own natural desire to learn. Mainstream education pushes the idea that the best way for children to learn something is to be drip-fed snippets of information on a subject every single day, gradually increasing in difficulty. They are then tested on their knowledge and if they pass a box is ticked and the subject is no longer explored.

Can you imagine a world where children were encouraged to seek out answers for themselves? Instead of being told to 'put down their hands' and not ask questions, they were encouraged to dive deep into their passions and question everything. Can you imagine a world where people believed that children had to power to learn everything they need to know on their own? Well, that my friends, is our world. That is unschooling.

# "SOMETIMES YOUR ONLY AVAILABLE TRANSPORTATION IS A LEAP OF FAITH"

*margaret shepard*

# INTO THE UNKNOWN

Choosing to live a life without school will really plunge you into an unknown abyss as a parent. You are going against the grain, willingly pursuing a life that is on the outside of what society expects. That requires a lot of grit and mental strength. Be prepared for a huge dose of self-doubt and questioning of your choices. This, unfortunately, is a side effect of unschooling that you are just going to have to learn to navigate.

Sometimes you will get a panicky feeling. You will ask yourself many questions. "Have we made the right choice to home educate our children?" "Am I doing enough?" "Are they missing out on things?" "Are they socializing enough?".

These are just some of the questions that creep into the sub-conscience. It's normal to feel this way. You're seeing people live their lives within the realm of "normal". You'll open your social media and see a picture of Susan's child holding a "superstar" award for getting 10/10 on her spelling test. That's awesome, well done Susan's kid! Do not let this detract from why you have chosen to unschool. You have chosen to ditch the rewards system for a childhood of freedom.

On the surface it may look like Susan's child is achieving more than your child. But before you even begin that nasty comparison game, remember you yourself have been conditioned all your life to compete with others, to compare your wins and successes to the wins and successes of your peers.

In order to unschool your children without the crippling self-doubt and green-eyed comparison getting you down you first need to undo and pick apart the years of social conditioning you yourself received as a child. Only then will you stop the niggling feelings of guilt. A feeling that somehow you will fail your children, that somehow you will let them down.

The first step into navigating this road is to unlearn the way you have been taught that children learn. I talked in an earlier chapter about how children are born with a natural desire to learn, to know everything about all the things.

*Learning isn't something that we do to children.* Learning is a natural process that happens all on its own. And when you realise this it opens the door to a whole new kind of education. The freedom and power to learn what they want, when they want and own it. To create the terms of their education; that is a beautiful gift to give your children. And a beautiful gift to give yourself; living this life alongside them, watching their learning unfold is truly an honour.

Once you realise that you don't need to "teach" your children in the traditional sense of the word. That you personally don't have to know all the things about all the stuff. Some of the massive pressure will be alleviated and home-schooling your children won't feel anywhere near as daunting. Do you know what? It's actually pretty fun. There's no need to teach; give them the freedom to teach themselves.

I know what you're thinking "that sounds awesome, but how do you make sure they're actually learning stuff and not just choosing to watch TV all day?".

It's quite simple really. Your role as the parent in an unschooling family is to facilitate. You are the master of inspiration, the involver. A curator, full of wonder, joy, and passion. This isn't as complicated as it sounds, I promise.

The easiest way to get started with this is to involve. Involve your children in everything that it is physically possible to involve them in. Off shopping? Help them to write or draw a list (ability dependant), give them their own money, help them to figure the shop out when you get there. Perhaps you're doing some cooking, let them help, try not to worry about the mess - you can enlist their help cleaning this up later. Need to clean the house, ask them to give you a hand.

Gardening, chores, life. Let them be a participant in daily life. This is honestly the best tool for learning. So often children are separated from the day to day stuff, let them in on it. Let me tell you a secret. If you stop giving children chores and teaching them that the day to day life admin is "hard" and "boring", choosing instead to share it with them, allowing them the choice to help you and participate. They will gladly help and feel chuffed to bits that you trust them.

Instead of; *"I have so much housework to do. Here's your list of chores, make sure they're done or no TV."*

Try; *"The house needs a bit of a clean; would you mind giving me a hand please then we'll have time to watch TV later?"*

Don't make life a game of "them" (children) and "us" (adults). We're all working together in an equal balance, sharing the roles and responsibilities.

Involving children in daily life is the first step, the next is to inspire them to learn. It sounds like a ton of effort I know, but it's really not, inspiring children is easy peasy.

Provide them with a stimulating environment to learn. Curate a collection of beautiful books. Watch documentaries with them. Talk to them often, read to them more. Take them to places of wonder. Get outside in nature. Socialise with a diverse range of people. Let them play.

Do this and you'll be winning. Do all of this and just watch the magical process of learning unfold.

You see learning isn't about finding answers it's about asking questions. As the facilitator your role isn't to answer the questions, your role is to guide your children to find the answers out for themselves. Children adore the trust that you afford them by allowing them to figure things out. They also feel a huge sense of pride and accomplishment when they've managed to do something independently, I mean don't we all?

Children also find a lot of joy when you are learning and discovering alongside them. It smashes the hierarchy that you get in school. School really devalues children. The idea that 'we', as adults, know best, know everything, have nothing to learn from 'you', children. It takes away children's inner power and they become reliant on hearing information from others and taking that as gospel. As a result, they lose their ability to question and find out information for themselves.

Not answering children's questions for them also gives them the opportunity to naturally expand on their learning.

For example,

*"Mummy, what is the biggest snake in the world?"*

"I'm not sure where could we find that out?"

*"In my big animal book?"*

"Great idea let's go fetch it and see if we can find the answer together."

*"Mummy, it says here the biggest snake in the world is the anaconda"*

"Where does it live?"

*"It shows a map, what country is that mummy?"*

"It doesn't say. Let's see if we can find that country on your globe."

*"Found it! What is it called?"*

"Well, that is the continent of South America, which is made up of lots of different countries."

*"Which ones mummy?*

"Let's have a look in the atlas shall we?"

*"Wow, this one is big, it's called Brazil. Isn't the rainforest in Brazil? Do you think that is where the anaconda lives? What does it eat?"*

<u>**"I'm not sure, shall we have a look together?"**</u>

As you can see, once you unlock that little curious mind the questions pour out of them. This forms the basis for all of your unschooling; questions, questions, questions. Solving the riddles of our world, together.

The struggle with natural, self-directed learning is that you can't measure it. This is probably the reason that schools don't allow it despite an abundance of evidence that it the best way of learning both for the academic success and mental wellbeing of the child. This is where your self-doubt and worry will creep in again.

There are no tests in unschooling or a tool to measure how much your child knows. This can be a worry when you know that they 'should' be able to do certain things by a certain age. Remind yourself, that there is no age when things 'should' be known. All humans learn things at their own pace, and the milestones created for school assessments are just that; created. Created by a group of powerful people to fit an agenda. It is worth reminding yourself of this often.

Learning in school is done in a very linear way. You learn a topic, you cover it once and it is checked off. You don't ever go back to that topic in all of your 13 years at school again. You never build on that knowledge.

Unschoolers tend to learn things in a much more fluid way. It can look erratic, compared to the orderly fashion things are taught in school, but actually when you dissect it and delve in it makes way more sense.

One day they will be engrossed in a particular skill or topic. Everything will be based around this for a sustained period of time. Then they'll drop it, seemingly no longer interested as they move on to another area of learning. Time will pass with lots of topics, skills, and interests having come and gone. Then one day they'll spark interest in a previous topic again. Only now, time has passed for them to make sense of what they have learned, they seem experts and you'll be amazed by how much information they have retained. This time they'll hone their skills and build on the information they learnt before. This seems to be the cycle of natural learning, the wheel of knowledge keeps turning, and they keep building on it as they grow.

Trust, kindness and a whole heap of patience thrown in is the recipe for success. Trust that your children are capable little humans, and trust that you are capable of building an environment where they can thrive. Be kind on yourself, stop the guilt you are doing enough by just being there and supporting your children on their learning journey. Be patient, sometimes it will look like they're not learning anything and you're not doing enough, but on the inside, a whole heap of wonderful learning is happening and they will floor you with their knowledge.

Most of all, remember why you're unschooling and what is important to you. My 9-year-old daughter couldn't tell you what a compound sentence is, but she could talk to you for hours about the civilisations of the ancient world, the exploitation of Asian elephants, how volcanoes are formed and the complex ecosystem of the Mariana trench.

You need to remind yourself often that your children are making progress every day. It may not be progress in terms of hitting government created academic targets. But they are progressing into free-thinking, creative, motivated, emotionally intelligent, kind human beings. They are unique, they are free.

# PART TWO: THE HOW

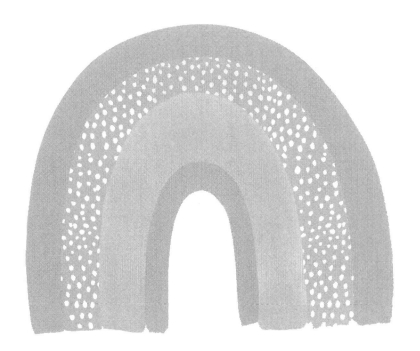

"PERHAPS PLAY WOULD BE MORE RESPECTED IF WE CALLED IT SOMETHING LIKE "SELF-MOTIVATED PRACTICE OF LIFE SKILLS," BUT THAT WOULD REMOVE THE LIGHT-HEARTEDNESS FROM IT AND THEREBY REDUCE ITS EFFECTIVE-NESS. SO WE ARE STUCK WITH THE PARADOX. WE MUST ACCEPT PLAY'S TRIVIALITY IN ORDER TO REALIZE ITS PROFUNDITY"

*peter gray*

# PLAY ALL DAY

I am a massive advocate for play. In my opinion, children should be free to spend their whole childhood immersed in an imaginary world of play. In fact, I'm going to be as bold as to say that more adults should spend time playing, maybe then the world would be a little brighter.

Most people who know us, know that our children spent 90% of their time playing. Most of the same people see this as a bad thing. "How can the children be learning when all they do is play all day?". And that my friends is the problem. Most adults don't really understand play, they don't know what real play is, therefore, they have created a clear line between learning and play. When, in actuality, the two things are not separate at all.

To understand play, real meaningful child-led play, you first need to look at the science behind it. Play is a crucial part of human learning and development, and it is all to do with something called counterfactual thinking. Counterfactual thinking is a concept in psychology that involves the human tendency to create possible alternatives to life events that have already occurred; something that is contrary to what actually happened in real life.

Einstein once said that "Play is the highest form of research" and he was absolutely correct. Scientific studies of play have actually found that children who spend more time playing are better at counterfactual thinking, meaning that they can think about different outcomes and possibilities. They can predict events and have better reasoning skills. When you dissect this further and think about the ways in which humans learn, it is truly fascinating stuff. Children are just like scientists testing different theories through their play. They imagine different ways the world around them could work and predict patterns of data that would follow if their theories were to come true. They then compare this pattern to the pattern of real-world events from their lives.

So now we understand the science and psychology of why play is so important we can start to think about what play actually is. The best way to do this is to think about what play is not.

Play is not something that can be done to the child, much like learning. Play is not adult-led. Play is free, it is child-led and it is fun. If you are setting up a "play-based" activity and leading the child through it with learning objectives in mind. THAT IS NOT PLAY. Sure, it's a fun activity to do together, and I'm all for doing these educational activities with your children (if they want to – no forced learning here thank you very much), but it isn't real meaningful play. Got it? Good!

Making time and space in your days for free play isn't just vital for the brain development of your child, it has so many benefits. When children play they are invoking all of their senses and using all of their bodies.

Some of the hidden benefits of play include:

- Physical wellbeing.
- Improves their fine motor skills.

- Enables critical thinking.

- Enhances their creativity.

- Increases concentration.

- Develops empathy and social skills.

- And most importantly, it brings immense joy to the child!

Contrary to popular belief children don't need an abundance of the latest toys to experience meaningful play. Some of my children's most memorable play experiences have been with sticks. Children will play with anything. In New Delhi we met a little boy who had made a car from some rubbish he had found on the street, he was so happy and really immersed in his play. So please don't think you need to bankrupt yourself to provide play experiences for your children. I would say quality over quantity every time.

Play is the foundation of unschooling that provides the basis for all of your children's learning opportunities. Play is so valuable and makes for a beautiful childhood. Make time and space for play, your children and you will reap the benefits.

# "CHILDREN ARE MADE READERS ON THE LAPS OF THEIR PARENTS"

*emilie buchwald*

# BOUNTIFUL BOOKS

In mainstream schooling, literacy is at the forefront of education from the moment a child begins school at the tender age of 4. From the minute they start school they are taught to read using the phonics system, then subsequently tested and measured on their reading skill. By age 8 all UK school-aged children are expected to be reading quite substantial chapter books and be able to spell words such as 'picturesque', 'consequence' and 'phenomenal' during weekly tests. They must learn about fronted adverbials and conjunctions. As well as writing large amounts comprehensively, in cursive writing, and being assessed termly. If they fall behind, they are taken out of other more creative lessons for 'interventions' to ensure they are not falling behind. All normal stuff for schooled children.

Now ask yourself, who made these targets? Who decided what our children should know and when they should know it by? Who do all of these data and assessments really benefit? Why do 8-year-olds need to know about fronted adverbials?

And the big question, what about children who are less academically gifted? The wild children, the free spirits. The painters, dancers, sportspeople and eccentric inventors.

Where do they fit into this one size fits all curriculum?

I can tell you. They have no place. They are forgotten, pushed to the back of the class. Told they are too chatty, too fidgety, too giggly, too naughty, too shy, too quiet, never contributing to class, told they are not good enough, told their best attempts at following instructions are wrong.

The consequences of being pushed to read and write before they are ready can be truly detrimental to not only a child's ability to read but also their mental wellbeing. I should know, it happened to our daughter. She developed a newfound hatred of reading at school because she was no longer reading for pleasure. She lost her confidence, feeling like she wasn't good enough, and even worse it eventually caused her mental health to suffer when she developed anxiety. Sadly, my daughter is not an isolated case.

In an ideal world, the one size fits all phonics system would be scrapped in favour of allowing children to first gain a love of reading and experiencing beautiful books of their choosing.

Pushing children to read and write too soon is extremely damaging and new scientific research has proven the fact.

Did you know that the right side of our brains develops first? The right side is the creative side, the emotional side, where imagination thrives and empathy develops. The left side of the brain is the analytical side, for problem-solving. The right side of the brain is usually developed by age 3 – 4, whereas the left side of the brain develops much later aged around 7. Do you see where I am going with this?

The left brain deals with language, numeracy, literacy, and time. It's the logical, calculating, planning part of us that keeps us centred in the 'real' world, present, past and future. The right brain takes care of our empathy, intuition, imagination, and creativity. It is where we believe, dream, imagine, feel and come alive. The left brain wants the end result, whereas the right brain only cares about the process of how we get to the end result.

The most important piece of this puzzle is the difference between the right brain and the left brain. The right brain is what makes us human beings, the left brain is only interested in the processing or the 'doing'. That is why we are called human beings, not human doings. We are not robots. If you watch very young children closely that are quite happy just 'being' and far less interested in 'doing'.

All of this science is why we need to be super careful about the timing of pushing academic learning. Pushing children to live in their left brains before they are ready can cause severe learning difficulties, as well as damage their mental wellbeing. They are forced to find the product (left brain) before they truly understand the process (right brain). They can develop something called "learned stupidity." This is where a child believes themselves to be incapable thereby losing their natural desire to learn.

This is exactly what happened to our beautiful, vivacious, imaginative daughter! She believed herself to be incapable and lost her natural desire to learn.

So 4 long years ago we pulled her out of school and began the long process of letting her grow to love learning again through our unschooling life.

This has been a long, arduous journey that has taken time and patience, but to witness the natural learning process that all children are capable of is really a magical sight to behold.

When she first left school we decided to take the pressure off completely. No forced reading, no coercion, no reward charts and definitely no boring phonics books. The goal for us was for her to learn to love reading again. We carried on reading a wide, varied selection of books to her every day. We made sure she witnessed us reading, and not just books, magazines, newspapers, signs.etc. We started the weekly tradition of 'Poetry Tea Time' where we'd huddle up with cakes and tea whilst reading poetry. Audiobooks are played in the background whilst we go about our daily lives. As well as weekly visits to bookshops and libraries.

By allowing her to grow in her own time, and fostering a nurturing environment where reading is seen as something to enjoy and take pleasure in, as opposed to something you are forced to do and tested on, she has started to pick up books and read. All by herself.

She can read at any time of the day, and can choose any books she wants; no longer restricted to a specific set of levelled books. Her books of choice at the moment are Shakespeare, (no joke!).

We have always been a family of readers and I am a self-certified book hoarder. Every day since the birth of our children I have read to them. This is just the story of our eldest daughter and her learning journey. Our youngest daughters reading journey was quite the opposite.

She could read fluently by the age of 5, at age 6 was already reading complex chapter books. Completely self-taught.

How? By fostering and modelling a love of reading, surrounding her with beautiful books and written words. Reading aloud a wide, diverse range of different texts to her several times a day.

Now I'm not trying to say that in doing this you too will have fluent readers by the age of 5. What I am saying, based on my experience is that children will develop their own reading skills when they are ready. My youngest daughter was ready at 5, my eldest still isn't there yet at 9. That's ok. Focus on the right brain, the left brain will catch up. Grow a love of reading before you push them to read to themselves.

Please don't feel overwhelmed, there are some really lovely, simple ways to introduce more reading into your days. You don't need to spend a fortune on Instagram worthy books.

- Incorporate library visits into your week.

- Choose books about your child's interests or hobbies.

- Read aloud over breakfast.

- Listen to audiobooks whilst going about your day or on long journeys.

- Read to your children whilst they are playing, having a bath (in fact squeeze reading in wherever you can)

- Let your children choose the books they want to read.

- Don't correct them when they are reading to you unless they ask you to.

- Read a wide variety of genres.

- Model a joy of reading to them.

- Let them see you reading everything (labels, letters, newspapers, magazines, lists, anything, and everything).

- Bring the stories to life with story baskets and imaginary play.

The greatest gifts you can give your family are a library card and quiet moments together hiding within the pages of beautiful books you have borrowed.

Above all else don't worry about academic goals, stop panicking about when they will learn to read. Let's trust our brilliant capable children, they'll learn what they need to when they need it.

"EVERY CHILD IS AN ARTIST. THE
PROBLEM IS HOW TO REMAIN
AN ARTIST ONCE WE GROW UP"

*pablo picasso*

# ARTY FARTY

Sir Ken Robinson advocates that "Creativity is as important as literacy". We have found this to be so very true. Creativity underpins all of their learning and allows humans to express themselves freely. This freedom to express themselves, to not be judged, to process thoughts, to foster their imaginations is so very important. We spend all day telling stories, playing and re-enacting stories. Any form of art is just an extension of the mind, a way for children to channel themselves.

Art lays the foundations for emotional development in children. By manipulating drawing tools and paintbrushes, their fine motor skills improve. Children who experiment with materials alongside learning shapes, colours, and mixing are learning the basics of scientific discovery and maths. More importantly, when children feel happy and good whilst they are creating their self-confidence is being boosted. Art gives children the freedom to experiment, make mistakes and invent new ways of creative and critical thinking.

I am a huge believer that you do not need to have an enormous amount of money to be able to home educate. Children actually want for very little and you can absolutely unschool on a tight budget. But, art is an area where you may need to loosen the purse strings a little. Having a wide and varied assortment of art materials available will only go to broaden your child's knowledge and creativity. Although saying this, these do not have to cost the earth. We live in an era of abundance and art materials can be picked up quite cheaply. It is also worth checking out charity shops and online selling sites, as well as local schools who sometimes have a clear out. In the past, we have asked for specific, pricier creative materials as gifts for the children from relatives as we feel they are more valuable than toys.

Leave these materials out in an area where you don't mind mess so children can access them easily whenever inspiration strikes. Some art materials we like to have to hand are:

- Pencils
- Pencil Crayons
- Watercolour palette
- Liquid watercolours
- Oil pastels
- Chalk pastels
- Wax crayons
- Glue
- Collage materials (old magazines, photos, greetings cards, fabrics)
- Paintbrushes, water pots, and mixing palettes
- Loose paper and card
- A spiral-bound sketchbook

- Fineliner pens

- Scissors

- Stamps

- Ink

These form the main basis of our art supply which is kept on a trolley where the children can access it whenever they need to. Occasionally we will buy something specialist or seasonal as an extra treat to add to the trolley. I am a firm believer in giving children access to all of the above (supervised as is age-appropriate) from the moment they can hold a pencil. There is nothing more magical than watching a baby discover paint for the first time and smear it all over themselves in an abundant act of pure joy.

As well as providing the materials for your mini artists it is also so important for you to inspire creativity. Firstly you should be prepared for a mess. Set up an art space where your children can be free to experiment without you or them worrying about ruining their clothes or your floor. Worry really stifles creativity.

It's really important that you don't direct your child when they are creating. This happens in school, at the end of a school day, the teacher is left with 30 identical paintings. The only way to differentiate is to read the names on the back, which most the class always forget write. We're trying to promote individuality here not copy famous artistic works. So instead of asking your child to paint something specific, just leave them to get on with it. If you wanted a picture of sunflowers, don't ask your child to paint sunflowers. Show them pictures of sunflowers, leave some out in front of your child whilst they're painting. Talk about the sunflowers together and show them Van Gogh's famous piece. Then step back, and see what they create.

Try not to create alongside your child unless they ask you to. It can be frustrating to a child if you're both drawing the same thing. They can either copy you, or feel inferior that their picture doesn't look like yours. Although some children do enjoy creating with you modelling how to do it, just get their consent first and judge their mood, you don't want to put them off.

Be specific when you discuss artwork with your children. Avoid comments like "that looks pretty". Instead, try "I really like your picture, why did you choose those colours? Which brush did you paint with? I like the strokes you made with your brush." Ask them deep questions such as, "Tell me about your picture." And "How did you feel when you made this?".

Learn to let go of perfectionism and let things be. You may not understand all of the art your child creates, it may look like nothing to you, but mean everything to them. Don't ever say things like "Have you finished, you've left lots of white paper that side?" or "Maybe you rushed it, it looks like you haven't finished.". Art is just as much about the process as it is about the finished article.

Developing your child's creativity isn't just about art. It incorporates drama, music, and dance too.

Other ways we encourage our children to be creative is playing many genres of music whenever we can, even on low in the background, it's still sinking in. This encourages them to dance too.

One of our family treats is sometimes we like to have a mini disco.

We turn off all the lights except a fancy disco lightbulb and choose our favourite music to dance around the living room together. Making beautiful childhood memories, that is at the heart of unschooling.

The children are pretty good at the drama part without our intervention now, they are always putting on plays for us. This has been developed over the years and begins with great storytelling, lots of imaginative play, role-playing and dressing up. Puppet theatres and doll theatres have been played with lots in our house. We also take them to the theatre, watch theatre and ballet on the TV and read them scripts.

Art, play, learning whatever labels you want to give the things your child gets up to, they all carry the same principles when we talk about unschooling, and as you progress through this book you will notice a couple of things. 1. Like I said at the start, unschooling is most definitely not unparenting. You will realise how heavily involved you are in raising your children. 2. Children are incredibly capable of learning everything they need to know when they need to know it, you just have to trust them.

I deeply encourage you to think about a childhood where art materials were treated as important as toys. Where children were free to create and express themselves every day. Wouldn't that be the most awesome thing? Imagine the adults they would become.

# "I HAVE DECIDED TO STICK WITH LOVE. HATE IS TOO GREAT A BURDEN TO BEAR."

*martin luther king jr*

# WONDERFUL WORLD

It would be irresponsible for me to write this book and not address the important issues facing our world today, and how we handle these when raising our children. I truly believe, along with many other unschoolers, that raising the next generation is the biggest catalyst for social change. We are facing unsettling times ahead and how we raise our children can greatly impact upon the future of our world. In my opinion, mainstream school is not doing a good enough job of this at present. This is closely linked to the fact the schools are controlled by governments, meaning curriculums are heavily influenced by current policy and agenda. This isn't a book about politics so I'll spare you my opinions on that one! The point I am trying to make here, albeit heavy-handedly, is that the narrative we feed our children about the world around us and the diverse people in it will greatly influence the adults they become.

The curriculum in schools is incredibly whitewashed. What I mean by this is that it teaches a very one-sided, male-dominated, white-centric narrative favoured by the western world. The British Empire is glorified with no mention of the colonisation that occurred in order to have an empire built on the backs of slaves. The slaughter of Native Americans is barely mentioned.

In geography, you learn about low economically developed regions with no mention of the exploitation of these countries by the more developed ones. I could go on, but I assume you get the picture by now.

Often people are not even aware that this is an issue. It is what is taught, what has always been taught, so it must be what is best. I favour uncomfortable truth over whitewashing. We want our children to understand the sacrifices that have been made to get where we are now in the world. Only by knowing the truth of things can we prevent the same mistakes happening over and over again.

I also think it is incredibly important to constantly check our privilege. We are a white, western family, my children were already ten steps ahead in life at birth than most due to this fact. It is important they know this so they can grow up treating others with respect and humility. Using their inherent privilege for good, as a platform to promote change.

Although we are not religious ourselves, we introduce them to all religions, take them to different places of worship and meet with people with different values and belief systems.

It is also important to talk to your children about LGBTQ people. Teach them that love is love, and people are all the same on the inside and therefore worthy of the same rights and respect as everyone else.

Introduce your children to differently-abled people, show them what it means to live a life being disadvantaged. Help them to understand so they will become more understanding.

Some ways we do this is by reading them books and watching

movies with a diverse range of characters. But the biggest way we help them understand diversity is communication. Communication with us, and communication with a diverse range of people.

When discussing bigger issues like the climate crisis, endangered species and the exploitation of third world countries, we always make it age-appropriate. We don't want to terrify them, so avoid comments like "The world will end in 8 years if we don't stop pollution", or something as equally morbid. Remember, children are like sponges they soak up everything they hear. Model good eco-friendly practice, read books and watch documentaries. Just don't go in too deep too soon.

We recently participated in some of the climate marches with the children and they adored it, feeling part of something bigger and the hope that brings that they are facilitating change. That's powerful for children. Give them the tools to be activists for issues they are passionate about. Help them to write to people in power, listen to their concerns, protest with them if that's what they want. You are your child's biggest advocate.

Obviously, make sure you are being age-appropriate when you discuss complex world issues with your children and answer their questions. You know them better than anyone, so know how much they can handle.

Children are not born prejudiced, uncaring people that is something they develop from influences around them. Be a positive influence so we can heal the world.

"TEACHING CHILDREN ABOUT THE NATURAL WORLD SHOULD BE SEEN AS ONE OF THE MOST IMPORTANT EVENTS OF THEIR LIVES"

*thomas berry*

# WILDLINGS

So many humans are disconnected from our natural world, and in this digital age where we are reliant upon screens, it seems more important now than ever to raise our children in nature, fostering a love of being outdoors and caring for the natural world around them.

The main most obvious way to encourage your child to learn to love nature is to let them spend as much time in it as possible in all weathers. If my children don't get outdoors every day they are literally climbing the walls by the time evening rolls around.

Forest schools are amazing and I highly recommend you find one. But they can be pricey, going on a nature walk is just as valuable. As is going to the beach, taking a picnic to a nature reserve, hanging out in the woods, cycling along a river, going on a hike. The world is quite literally your oyster here.

If your lucky enough to have your own garden, grow some plants with your children. Even better, grow some fruit and vegetables with them. They love the process of farm to fork. Don't panic if you don't have a garden. Lots of places have community gardens you can volunteer to get involved in or allotments. Maybe an elderly neighbour needs help tending to their garden. Use your initiative, social media is your best friend here.

I know the weather can be off-putting, but unless it is dangerous, make the effort to head on outdoors. Invest in some wet weather gear, puddle jumping with your children brings so much joy. Remember you're creating a childhood full of memories for them. Enjoy it.

Create a space in your home for nature. We have a nature table. The children are the curators and collect natural things of interest such as feathers, eggshells, leaves, flowers, stones, sticks, and beach finds. We have nature posters on the wall, a microscope and some nature books. I tend to swap these around with the changing of the seasons. It doesn't have to be fancy if you don't have space, a shelf or basket would do. The most important thing is to ensure that your children are curating the space. They decide what lives where in the nature area.

We also like to go on a nature walk each week. The children have a small sketchbook that we use as a nature journal. They write in the weather, draw anything of note, maybe glue in some pressed flowers. It's a fun, cute little tradition with lots of open-ended ways to explore nature further.

My biggest tip when exploring nature with your children is to let them take risks. Allow them to climb trees, dig in the dirt, run around in a state of undress. Don't project your fears onto your children. Internalise them and let them play and explore. Children are naturally curious about their environment, we need to encourage that curiosity by allowing them to explore and learn. Risky play is incredibly important for childhood development. Society is building fences and walls around children by encouraging you to restrain and hover over their every move. Step back, trust them. Sometimes they'll fall, they'll get hurt, accidents happen. You support, commiserate, build on and move on.

I mean, don't even get me started on running up the slide! It's ok people, there isn't some warped playground police that will take away your children for going up the slide instead of down.

We wonder why children are growing up to be less and less creative, restricting their curiosity and desire to explore the natural world around them will only hinder their future growth. Let them roam, let them play, let them unleash the wildling buried deep within them.

# "LIFE ITSELF IS YOUR TEACHER, AND YOU ARE IN A STATE OF CONSTANT LEARNING"

*bruce lee*

# SCREENTIME

I have spoken so much about ways to connect with our children in a world of disconnect but haven't really touched on a large part of our unschooling philosophy, the source of disconnect; screens.

Screentime is the biggest parenting minefield out there. Ours is the first generation of children that are growing up with huge advances in technology shaping their everyday lives. Due to this, there is very little evidence out there to help guide us when navigating the digital world with our children.

I cannot tell you what is best here. It is a deeply personal area, therefore you need to do your own research. We're all learning together. I can only share our story in the hope that it may shed some light on these murky waters.

We didn't share any pictures of our children on social media until last year. In fact, we didn't have any social media accounts up until 2 years ago, it didn't fit with our jobs and lives at that time. I actually joined social media when I began home educating the girls as a way to connect with other families, social media is fabulous for meeting like-minded souls. But I am not naïve I know the risks and the dark side of the internet. Consent plays a huge role in our lives. We always get the girls consent before doing anything, including posting about them online.

Up until last year, the only photographs of our children online were photos of the backs of their heads. Last year, when I launched my blog and our travels became news, we had to chat with our children about sharing online. We talked about the positive side of social media, and also what it means to share a photo online. They watched some travel families with us and decided they would like to be a part of sharing our story. Our reasoning for this is that it is inevitable that one day in the future our children will want to have a social media account. We are hoping that by showing them how to use it responsibly and share appropriately we can model best practices to them and avoid the cyberbullying and awkward 'duck pout' selfie stage that many teenagers go through. Again, we have no evidence for this, it's all so very new. Consent is key, so before we share we show them our planned post, talk about why we're sharing and get their consent to share. It's a long, awkward process, but I'd hate for them to be mad about any pictures I posted of them when they are older.

YouTube is a huge source of parental worry for us and something that we do restrict. I once read that you are only 3 clicks away from something dodgy on YouTube. We do let them watch YouTube videos that we have sourced and pre-approved for them. It's such a useful learning tool with some fantastic videos. I know it sounds strict, but you wouldn't let them watch an 18 certificate movie, so why would you give them free rein on an app that has unregulated 18 content able to slip past the tightest parental control settings? It makes no sense to me.

Tablets are also a fantastic learning resource, as are some video games. It's also about balance. Our girls each have a kindle tablet. I keep the security settings tight and download age-appropriate games, apps, and books.

We don't restrict the use of these tablets, not wanting to make them forbidden fruit. Do you know what? They rarely play on them. I don't believe that children are addicted to screens, or naturally want to choose screen time over and above everything else. I believe that often it is a lack of connection and other stimuli that drives children to use screens, but that fact is a little too close to home for some parents to stomach, so the addiction narrative is easier to go along with. Our children get plenty of connection and other stimuli, so choose that over screens, every, single, time.

We also love documentaries, fun tv shows and movies as a family. Often though we are too busy enjoying the simpler things in life to make time for binge-watching TV. But again it's not restricted.

One thing we do insist on for all of us is no screens during mealtimes or an hour before bed. This rule is for us adults more than the kids though!

Technology is amazing, and it is the future. It is so important that our children are computer literate so they can navigate this ever-evolving digital world. By modelling appropriate use of screens, and guiding them to make good choices online we can hopefully ease them into the complex space that is the internet.

"THE IDEA THAT CHILDREN NEED TO BE AROUND MANY OTHER YOUNGSTERS IN ORDER TO BE 'SOCIALISED' IS PERHAPS THE MOST DANGEROUS MYTH IN EDUCATION AND CHILD REARING TODAY"

*dr raymond moore*

# SOCIALISATION

"But what about socialisation?" = The number one question that parents who home educate their children are asked time and time again. To be honest I get really fed up with the ridiculousness of this question now. So much so that I often feel like replying with "I'm not sure socialisation means what you think it means" or "Well you attended school and you're clearly not very good at socialising". But, I'm not that rude (or brave!).

Socialisation was never something I worried about when we chose to home educate, I was more concerned with how badly I'd mess up my kids (joking). Maybe, that's just because I understand what socialisation is.

In mainstream school socialising isn't natural. Think about it for a moment and it all starts to seem a little weird. Children are put into a class with 29 other children who are all exactly the same age, within this class they are separated into groups based on academic ability, sometimes also based on gender. For an hour a day, they are forced outside onto a concrete square and told they must play, again with children the same age as them.

Now ask yourself, when in your adult life have you ever been forced into a room with 29 other adults the exact same age as you, split into groups based on academic achievement/gender and told "You must play, make friends, play now!" I mean, come on, it's ridiculous. It sounds like some bizarre cult. This is what we call meaningful socialisation? I don't think so.

When I think about my children and the social interactions they have on a daily basis I'm am not worried in the slightest whether or not they are getting enough socialisation. They have good relationships with diverse people from birth to old age. The friendships they have with other home educated children are so wonderful. When they play with younger children the children tend to become very nurturing, gentle, playing a more motherly role. When they play with children older than them the children seem to observe, learn, and be inspired by them. They enjoy being both a role model for younger children and gleaning inspiration from the older ones.

Teaching children to socialise in a school setting means sticking a group of them together with no guidance other than punishment when they do the wrong thing. People don't learn socialisation from only people their own age, with the same level of social skills. Children learn from being guided and supported in social situations, and from watching older children and adults model appropriate behaviour and relationships.

If you don't send your child to school, most people think that they're missing out on important socialisation. The brutal social rituals of perpetuating shame that is commonly accepted in school culture are not ideals you want your children to conform to. What about the bizarre, twisted rites of passage? Bullying is almost accepted as something that everyone goes through, it toughens you up. Yet as adults we wouldn't accept bullying in the workplace. So why then is it OK for our children to experience it as part of school life? Games in the playground are played with themes of exclusion and power. These are all things I have never witnessed in our groups of home educated children, yet myself and others who have attended school are sadly all too familiar with.

It is often argued that children need to go to school because they need to learn how to live in the 'real world'. Another ridiculous assumption. Children who are home educated live and learn in the 'real world' all the time. How can learning through real-life experiences even compare to that of school?

If the social skills you want your children to learn are conformity, gossiping, bullying, competition, to lose their compassion and individuality then it seems that school is the place to be. We find that home educated children are doing just fine out here in the 'real world'.

When I have watched my children play with schooled children it has always been games that involve a sense of hierarchy. There is a pack mentality with one child assuming the role of Alpha. We've all witnessed this type of play, maybe even have memories of it when we were children. This mentality continues right into senior school, where you have well-established cliques and children feel they must hide their true selves in order to fit in and conform with the 'cool kids'. My daughter often came home from school crying because children had said things like "You can't play our game unless you know the password.", or "You can't play with us today there are already too many people".

I am yet to witness this type of play within our home educated communities. All the children look and act, different, they are free to express themselves fully and all the other children are accepting of this. When they play it is always on a level playing field without the need for a hierarchy. There is often one or two 'leader' figures but they seem to take into account everyone's values and opinions. There, of course, can be some conflict – that is human nature. But, the children are fabulous at conflict resolution and when left are great at working out a result that is inclusive to all. I liken it to a democracy, it's wonderful to watch.

I feel that rewards systems in school have much to blame for the bullying and dangerous hierarchy in the playground. A bold claim I know, but hear me out.

The correct name for using rewards and punishments to teach children is 'operant conditioning'. The idea behind it is that a behaviour that is rewarded is more likely to be repeated. It is how we train dogs and other animals. After generations of social conditioning, we now believe as a society that children also cannot learn without 'operant conditioning' – rewards and punishment. That's because it does work, really well actually.

For me, the problem is how 'operant conditioning' works when we use it on children. This type of reward system teaches a child to expect a reward in exchange for task completion or certain behaviour. The danger is when you stop rewarding the behaviours, there's a good chance it will go away. Another potential risk of using this method is that if you use it with your children,  eventually when you ask them to do something, they'll respond with "what do I get for it," or "what's in it for me?".

The reason for this is that in giving physical rewards for something, you are giving the child an 'extrinsic motivation' for the behaviour. Meaning that the motivation for doing the task is external, it is not driven by a child's desire to do it.

In mainstream education, researchers have found that intrinsic motivation is related to a child's natural desire to learn or motivation to learn for the sake of learning. Whereas extrinsic motivation is associated with performance goals or learning in the pursuit of evaluation, or a good grade; a reward. This is dangerous territory because it undermines the development of any internal, or intrinsic motivation to do the very same thing. In layman's terms if children are rewarded for doing well in school their motivation for learning will be completely based on receiving rewards, and not by any inherent appreciation for knowledge. It basically suppresses a child's natural desire to learn. Use this system for their entire school life and you can pretty much guarantee they will completely lose any natural desire to learn or intrinsic motivation to achieve.

Unintentionally and below the surface 'operant conditioning' pits children against one another. Children feel like the ones who receive the most rewards, are far more deserving and worthy. The children who receive the most praise have an air of privilege and entitlement which places them higher up in the hierarchy.

Controversial as this may seem; it is all quite basic human psychology. The subject of socialisation is always the hottest topic when home education is discussed. I feel that people know socialisation in school, like many things, doesn't work in the current system. I have read about some wonderful democratic schools where many age groups mix together and they don't have issues with bullying and competition. This is the future of learning. By unschooling your children you're just well ahead of the times.

There is also an assumption that siblings can't and don't want to be friends with one another, It's a sad fact that at school siblings are separated. Many hours of separation at school has a profound impact on their close bonds. It is widely accepted that they do not play together and would be embarrassed to acknowledge one another. From my experience, unschooling gives siblings a beautiful gift of friendship.

Unschooled siblings are one another's greatest allies, they spend hours immersed in magical imaginary worlds, helping one another, sharing joy and affection and making wonderful memories together. Siblings don't have to drift apart as they age, this isn't a natural growth, it is often that school interferes, It's impossible to be forced apart for most of your waking hours and still have a deep connection. Strong sibling bonds are just another reason why unschooled children don't suffer in terms of socialisation. In reality, they gain so much.

It may be a large worry when you choose to home educate, wondering how your children will socialise. Humans are naturally social by nature. As long as you are living your life to the full alongside your children they'll have wonderful social opportunities. Get yourself on social media. There is a large home ed community out there and events in most places every week that you can join. Also, don't feel like you can only socialise with home educated families. Our children attend the same after school activities as other children and have lots of friends who attend school. Children make friends much easier than adults by just playing with them. I know putting yourself out there can be scary, but just do it. You'll make some wonderful adult friends and your children will thank you in the future for being so very brave.

"THE QUESTION IS NOT, - HOW MUCH DOES THE YOUTH KNOW WHEN HE HAS FINISHED HIS EDUCATION - BUT HOW MUCH DOES HE CARE? AND ABOUT HOW MANY ORDERS OF THINGS DOES HE CARE? IN FACT, HOW LARGE IS THE ROOM IN WHICH HE FINDS HIS FEET SET? AND, THEREFORE, HOW FULL IS THE LIFE HE HAS BEFORE HIM?"

*charlotte mason*

# RHYTHM & FLOW

As I have said many, many (too many perhaps) times in this book unschooling is not 'unparenting'. It isn't about following a curriculum or strict routine, but this does not mean that you cannot find your own natural routines. The easy-going flow and rhythm to your days, weeks, months, seasons and years will come to underpin your child's unschooling education.

The key to finding a natural rhythm and flow that will work for your family is to keep it intentionally simple. Take off the pressure, learn to not feel guilty about having to say no to things, keep lots of time free for plans to change. Unschooled children can become deeply immersed in play or learning projects, give them free time for this.

We like to incorporate the ebb and flow of the seasons into our unschooling too. We do this with small gestures like changing up the books we're reading to seasonal ones, eating seasonal foods, getting outside more in spring and summer, slowly hibernating in autumn and winter.

I also find it's important to make time to prioritise everyone's individual needs during the week. This sounds tricky and can be a logistical nightmare to put into practice, but it's super important to maintain a happy balance to our family life. The children have their own hobbies and interests that they do separately giving them some alone time with their own separate friendship groups. We also make small moments of connection and 1:1 time with each child so they feel valued individually within our family unit. This can be as simple as a visit to the bookshop or bakery with one child or playing a game alone with them. It really does wonders for our family equilibrium.

One of the toughest parts of unschooling is finding time for self-care. You are with your children for the majority of your time. It is only natural that sometimes this will get too much, you will feel suffocated, over touched and craving some adult time. Make your self-care a priority, you cannot be fully present and patient with your children if you are feeling under the weather yourself. That old adage 'fill your own cup before filling others' is so true here. Ensure you carve out time for yourself to do something that fills you with joy and replenishes the batteries.

Find beautiful moments of connections and traditions to anchor your days. For us this is reading picture books over breakfast, reading poems every day over tea, cuddles and dreamy chapter books before bed. Weekly nature walks, children helping with the meal prep and chores. These are all small seemingly normal parts of life, but for us, they can be the most magical. These small tasks bring us great moments of joy and often spark the deepest, most meaningful conversations. It is in these quiet moments that we all fill one another's cups to bursting.

# "FIND SOMEONE WHO KNOWS YOU'RE NOT PERFECT BUT TREATS YOU AS IF YOU ARE"

*anonymous*

# TRUST

Trust and connection are the underpinnings of all familial bonds. They are particularly important when you unschool, you have to have so much trust, and work on your connections with your children every day. You also have to have heaps of trust in yourself and your decisions.

If you co-parent then making sure you're on the same page with your parenting and unschooling choices is of utmost importance, but this brings with it it's own trials and tribulations. Choosing to unschool challenges both parents parenting values. You have both had different upbringings with completely separate ideas about what constitutes 'good' parenting. Both parties have to work on unpicking their own ideals, values, conditioning, and upbringings, to do what they believe to be best.

Unschooling is not just a method of education it is a complete way of life. If one parent isn't really on board and you don't have a united front then you will come up against so many walls. The key, as with most parts of relationships is communication. Major discussions need to happen for you to fully understand each other and set the standards that you wish to parent by, together. My husband and I have many, many conversations deep into the night about how we parent our girls.

Occasionally we clash, it's inevitable this will happen. I may not be happy with how he has handled a particular situation, maybe he was too hot-headed, maybe he intervened sooner than I would have liked. Vice versa, he may not be happy with how I dealt with an issue or when I'm tired I can be very snappy and short with the girls. We throw our parenting values in one another's faces, it's life, it happens.

Kindness is key here. Remembering, that we're only human, humans who both want the same things for our children. Making time for one another to remember why we chose to live life as partners in the first place.

If you have a partner who isn't keen on the idea of unschooling, talk to them, explain the research and your reasons for wanting this lifestyle. If they still refuse to budge, then ask them why. Usually, it's because they don't really understand what it's all about and what it actually means for children, nor do they really understand how children learn. I always say if people do not take the time to read about it and form an opinion based on factual information, then they don't really get to have an opinion on that subject.

Quite often the underlying reason that people are so against unschooling, despite secretly wanting to, is fear. Fear of the unknown, and a fear of what other people may think of their choices. Honestly, I get it. We have had some major criticism from strangers and even close family. You have to learn just to deal with it. You're living life so outside of the ordinary that people don't understand it, and people often fear what they don't understand.

"DO WHAT YOU FEEL IN YOUR HEART TO BE RIGHT - FOR YOU'LL BE CRITICISED ANYWAY. YOU'LL BE DAMNED IF YOU DO, AND DAMNED IF YOU DON'T."

*eleanor roosevelt*

# QUIET THE NOISE

Most opinions surrounding parenting and educating other than at school, the most common questions, all stem from fears and doubts. Fears and doubts are normal, it's all part of the process of growing. People are supposed to grow and growth is meant to be uncomfortable.

What you may not expect as an unschooler is that at any social gathering and family event you can often be swarmed with questions and judgements about your life choices. Even a simple trip to the shop can end with a complete stranger firing sums at your children. No joke this actually happens.

Modern-day parenting is full of judgement and worries anyway. Throw into the mix your choice to unschool and you're really opening yourself up to criticism. Why people feel the need to question you and your children I will never understand, but sadly they do. My only advice is to brace yourself, learn to let it go over your head, be sure in your choices and have a supply of witty retorts ready for when random, rude questions are fielded your way.

Sometimes people are not meaning to be rude they are genuinely curious about what unschooling is and why you choose to live your lives that way. This is your opportunity to brag about how awesome unschooling is and share your knowledge.

Sadly, sometimes people are just rude, and really do believe that you are a) crazy and b) neglecting your children. I've done lots of work trying to figure out where this disdain comes from and I have come to one conclusion.

People are scared and jealous. They are scared of a life they don't understand. They are scared of the fact that you may have just found a better way to do life. The fact that they spent 13 years of their life being institutionalised can be a terrifying reality check. They can also be very jealous that you are brave enough to live life differently. To walk a road less travelled, free from the crushing expectations thrust upon you by society. It is worth bearing this in mind when you are confronted with judgement. I always consider two things when my decisions are being criticised and judged.

1.    Is it worth my time? 99.9% of the time the answer is no.

2.    Is that person living a life that I would want? Therefore, do I value their opinion?

Quiet the noise around you, remind yourself why you are choosing this. Nothing else matters except the happiness of your family unit.

# MANTRAS

To end, I'll leave you with reasons to choose unschooling if you don't already, or maybe let's call them mantras for you veteran unschoolers to remind yourselves why this lifestyle is so awesome.

- I want my children to learn how to learn, and be passionate about it.

- I want them to be free to express themselves and grow into who they're supposed to be without having to conform to societies expectations.

- I don't want them to grow up with fear as their biggest motivator.

- I want a slow joyful pace to our days.

- I want them to form deep connections with their family and friends.

- I want to cherish and protect their childhood.

# RECOMMENDED READING

These books have been invaluable for me when I feel like the overwhelm might just swallow me up whole.

FREE TO LEARN - PETER GRAY

HOW CHILDREN LEARN- JOHN HOLT

THE BRAVE LEARNER - JULIE BOGART

THE READ-ALOUD FAMILY - SARAH MACKENZIE

THE ENCHANTED HOUR - MEGHAN COX GURDON

NON VIOLENT COMMUNICATION - MARSHALL B. ROSENBURG

**And here are the sources of my research for this book.**

[1] YouGov: All figures, unless otherwise stated, are from YouGov Plc. Total sample size was 1250 education professionals. Fieldwork was undertaken between 9th-23rd June 2017. The survey was carried out online. The figures have been weighted and are representative of the UK teaching population by phase and region.
[2] Bentley, H. et al (2017) How safe are our children? The most comprehensive overview of child protection in the UK 2017
[3] The Key, a national school support service
[4] Association of Teachers and Lecturers
[5] NSPCC
[6] British Medical Journal
[7] Data from the Office for National Statistics

I'm Natalie, thank you for reading my book (hopefully it's the first of many more).

I'm 31, I drink 20384738 cups of tea a day (I may have exaggerated ever so slightly), I'm addicted to cake, books and our beautiful planet. Currently, I'm living in a camper van with my awesome husband William and our two feisty daughters. You see we had this crazy idea last year to sell our home, and it's contents, quit our jobs and use our savings to travel the world with the children.

We had four incredible months exploring South East Asia but sadly had to return to the UK as my husband had a tumour in his nose. The tumour turned out to be nothing too serious, so we bought a camper van, spruced her up, named her Wanda and set off in her for more family adventures.

If you want to see where this crazy life takes us then give me a follow on social media, I'd love to connect with you all. Also, feel free to email me if you have any questions about unschooling, life or you just want to chat about whether ginger cake tastes better than a lemon drizzle. I'm more of a seasonal cake eater, ginger cake in winter, lemon in the summer, oooh actually scones in the summer. I mean don't even argue with me about scones, jam first every time. Who puts cream on first? Sickos!

**BLOG: WILDWANDERINGTRIBE.COM**

**EMAIL: WILDWANDERINGTRIBE@GMAIL.COM**

**@WILD_WANDERING_TRIBE**

# GRATITUDE

I would like to give thanks to my family for always accepting me and allowing me to fill my head with dreams. In particular, my Mama who has stood by me through all my mistakes which have given her a fair few grey hairs over the years. I wouldn't be who I am without you. Thank you for always giving me your honest advice, even though I rarely choose to take it! And Daddy, I hope I'm doing you proud. One of the last things you ever said to me was "Always follow your heart my little treasure.". That changed me Pops.

My wonderful husband William. You are the only one who knows me inside out, the only one who never tells me that I can't do something. Thank you for having the faith in me to pursue our dreams and trusting that together we can make them come true. I know I'm a royal pain in the butt sometimes, you deserve a medal! You just get it, this life thing, I couldn't ask for a better human to do life with.

My beautiful, strong girls. You made me, my greatest teachers. Everything I do is for you my darlings. I hope one day you read this book and understand why we gave you the childhood we have. You bring me so much joy. Never stop dreaming little rebel girls of mine.

And finally, I want to thank myself, ha! I am a huge introvert and live my life in moments of perpetual solitude, alone with my thoughts, and worries, and crippling self-doubt. I am thankful and proud that I had the guts to quit my job and pursue my dreams, despite the world telling me not to. And I was brave enough to write and publish this book, even if no one reads it I feel proud that I dedicated my time and poured my heart onto this pages.

For all the women out there who feel different, alone, like they are never enough. Embrace it, own it and do whatever the hell you want. Life is too short not to!

**THIS BOOK HAS BEEN PRINTED ON RECYCLED PAPER**

Printed in Great Britain
by Amazon